The T

By Anne Marie Whalley

I dedicate *Tides of Life* to you, my grandchildren and future great grandchildren.
I came to the United States of America in 1990 with your grandfather, and I wish our descendants to always be proud of who they are and where they came from.

Forward

This collection of prose and poetry spans the years of the author and her recollections of life experiences. This book, written as a gift to her children and grandchildren, is written in a "French Style". You will hear the voice inflections are European. This collection is for anyone who feels life and love and family in a personal way.

Experience the life she had in France, where she was born, and America, where she resides today, through her words and the emotions behind them.

-Circe Denyer, writer, photographer

Preface

My ex-husband worked, played sports and bridge. He had little time for the children, or no time at all. He was very competitive. I found myself educating three daughters on my own. I loved it. I spoiled them a lot. In exchange they had to be very good at studying. They had also different activities. They practiced gymnastic, tennis, diving and piano. I was mostly on the road, driving them back and forth from home. We vacationed at Club Med for years. Through the company my ex worked for, we found a village under pine trees, with activities for children and adults. We went on vacation there for numerous years. The kids loved it. We did too.

The divorce happened and things changed dramatically.

The children started to rebel. Their grades at school went down. I worked. I was temporary for about two years and then I accepted a regular job because my manager was very professional. I met my new husband there. We moved to California after our wedding.

I was alone in our apartment while my husband worked. The children were at school. I drove my car very often to familiarize myself with the area.

America was very different from France. Everything was big. I had trouble adjusting to my new life. The first time I used a self-serve gas pump I got gasoline all over my legs. I went grocery shopping with a hand-written list. I had to take my driving test. The written part was difficult, but I passed the first time. Driving was fine. The next step was to learn how to drive the children back and forth to school. I made some new friends at the school. Most of them were French, working with the same company I used to work for in France.

From the apartment we moved to a big house. The children had their own bedrooms. Their grades were great. I was happy again. My husband began speaking about having our own company. I was scared. I had always worked with companies that had their own computer teams. What would I do if I had a problem when typing? Nobody would be with me to help me.

I learned how to use DOS and I did a great job formatting our documents. By hand, my husband wrote what I needed to type and we were a wonderful team. Having our company at home was tremendous hours of work. The fax rang at 2:00am or we sent faxes at that time of day.

I was now very comfortable in my new life. We invited friends over and I cooked French for them. I cooked French every day anyway. Groceries, cleaning, working, driving; I found myself really busy. The children were happy. My husband was happy with my work. He was always telling me that I was great. I believed him. We had fun.

It was not easy, but we made it. After a while we even had the chance to move our company outside our home. We succeeded. Did we do so for the education of our children?

Today we work at home again. The children love us; respect us. We see our grandkids very often. Could we ask for more? Except that we get older and we wish to be in good health.

This is a collection of prose and essays written with a touch of French thinking. Isn't it wonderful to feel free?

Acknowledgements

I would like to thank my creative writing class for supporting me every week in changing my life. The impact each of you has made has been tremendous.

Special Thanks to my teacher and friend, Judith Cassis. She gave me self-esteem. She encouraged me. Without her I would not have been able to have shared so completely from my heart.

Most of all, I thank my husband, Ron, who supported me and encouraged me in my writing adventure.

The Tides of Life

Mystery

Life is a mystery.
I am the last of fourteen.

I should not have been born.
Growing behind a tumor, I survived.

I came of very low birth weight.
I needed a blood transfusion right away.

I stayed two months at the hospital.
In cotton, I was fighting for my life.

Here I am today in the United States.
Who would have believed that?

He Walked Me to School

My dad was retired. He cultivated the garden.
He played a lot with me.

I did not want to go to school.
I loved the tranquility of the house.
Mom was cleaning, cooking, washing.

I loved to go and watch my dad in the garden.
I spoke to him and he gave me fruits to eat.
We also went for promenades together.

My brother and sisters were at school.
School started for me – day care.
I still remember my teacher.

She was young, nice. She smiled a lot.
It was a discovery for me.
I had preferred to stay home.

My father picked me up for lunch.
After lunch he tried to walk me back to school.
I was crying – I did not like the naps in the afternoon.

He carried me on his hips and walked me anyway.
Everyone in the village knew who was crying.
People spoke to my dad and me.
They were at their doors – with candies.

There were three grades in the same classroom.
I learned how to do my job and listen to the teacher.
I had known at an early age how to read and write.
What I loved were the promenades after school.

My sister and I were in the same school for girls.
We picked up my brother at the school for boys.
We had a snack that mother had prepared for us.

We walked for more than an hour.
We stopped by the soccer field.
We returned home, relaxed.
I learned to like school in the afternoon.

My Father

After school I did my homework with him.
I spoke to him. I played with his beret.
I was the only one permitted to do so.

The house was always filled with family.
My married sisters and brothers visited us often.
My friend's sisters and brothers did the same.

My brother and I played with our neighbors.
The house was small, but comfortable.
Dad had a little retirement.

One evening my young brother, sister and I
were called to our neighbor's house.

The day after, we went to kiss our father in his bed.
I thought that he was sleeping.

We stayed at our neighbor's house.
We went to school as usual.
We played with our friends.

Mom picked us up three days after.
Dad was not at home – I asked why.
"He is with Mary," said she.

I had no trouble understanding that.

I was looking for him to come back.
After a long while when at catechism,
I understood that I would not see him again on earth.
I cried for two years. I missed him.

Baby Doll

Never had a toy before; this one was precious.
I did not realize that she was not brand new.
I loved her right away; I became a mother that day.

I played with my baby doll.
I did not have her long enough.
It happened on a beautiful day....

We had a wood stove in the house.
Mom was busy cooking.
I was playing outside under a ladder.
The attic was above me.

My sister threw down some logs.
One came down ...Right on my baby's face.
My baby was broken.

I started to cry – not for long.
I kissed my baby doll good-bye.
My sister wanted to buy me another one.
I refused – that one was unique.

She would never find another one with that face.
My brother and neighbors were happy.
I was playing with them again.
Was I stubborn or simply hurt?

Shadows and Light

We were two young children.
We ran and played in the countryside.
We were happy and comfy.
Money was not a problem.
We did not have much.

The widow worked for the farmer.
In exchange she had seeds, animals.
We ate meat, vegetables and fruits.
Mother had a small retirement.
With it she could buy butter.
We were missing nothing;
Not even bread at the table.

Not a lot of conversation,
But laughter and smiles.
For us kids, books were our kingdom.

The electricity was missing.
An oil lamp was the light.
Mother cooked with a coal-fired stove.
The fireplace heated our home.

The ambiance was similar to that of some paintings.
The shadows and the light were our universe.
Our home was cozy, warm, and very old.
It was a meticulous feeling of wellbeing.

"The dinner is ready," said Mother.
No one heard her beautiful voice.
She approached us delicately.
She closed our books carefully.
We then set the table.

Christmas in France

It was following World War II that my parents educated fourteen kids. Being the baby, I was spoiled with love. No money could buy the feeling I had for my parents. The house was warm; always filled with plenty of kids and adults. My brothers and sisters lived not far away and Christmas; *Christmas,* what an enchanted event for me!

We began by having dinner together at my parents' house. We always had plenty to eat and the big breads on the table were magnificent. It was as if we were at a big reception. The house smelled of food from morning to evening and the pastries baking in the oven had an aroma I will not forget.

After dinner, we went to the procession before mass. The village people waited in line, letting the young kids go first. Then the priest came along with the altar boys. Following behind, the village people entered the very old church. Listening to the midnight mass, we sang songs of joy. When the mass ended we returned home. We children could not sleep awaiting gifts from Santa. We never saw him in our house and we had no idea how he looked, but on the morning of Christmas we always, always had a new pair of pajamas and one orange in our shoes. I remember that my parents had an onion in theirs.

Those pajamas were luxurious for us. We needed no gift wrap and every year it was a surprise for us (us being six children still at home.) I am so excited to write about Christmas as I have known it. I want forever to keep in my memories this warm, loving time of year.

Thank you, Mom and Dad, for giving us so much love and for keeping the mystery of Santa alive for so many years. I miss the orange in my shoes nowadays. I miss you too. You are always in my thoughts at Christmastime. Thank you also for the ritual of the midnight mass.

I need a new pair of pajamas for Christmas this year. I am wondering if Santa knows about it.

The Barn

We lived isolated from the village.
What I recall was me being afraid.

I could see the widow looking at the window.
I was, too. We saw a light.

Someone was in the barn.
I went to bed praying.

I was thinking of our mom.
What if something would happen to her?

I was scared for her;
Not for me.

Hospital in the Mid 50s

Never saw it before – No T.V. at home.
No money to go to the movie theatre.
My ear hurt – had to go to the hospital.

I had never left my mom before.
She left me in an unknown place.
I saw her leaving; saw her back.
She was walking toward the stairs.
I screamed – I cried – I was scared.
Nobody explained to me.

That place was big – I was left alone.
I still could see her back.
A sister saw me running after her.
She took me to a room with two beds.
This place was big – unknown.
I ran where ever I could see stairs.

A sister took me with her.
She took me into a room.
No electricity – no bed – dark room.
I was eleven years old.
I spent the night on the floor.
I was terrified – could not see a thing.
I cried all night long – silently.

In the morning a sister came.
She took me to a room.
I saw several people.
Nobody talked to me.
I was scared – could not move.
I was looking – observing – my ear hurt.

I woke up – did not know where I was.
I woke up thinking of the dark room.
My mom was beside my bed.
I was crying, but for joy.
A doctor spoke to her.

My ear did not hurt anymore.
My heart was bleeding.

My kids and I shared a room at the clinics.

Public School/Playfields

It was free and fun to learn.
He was in the boy's school and
I was in the girl's school.
The cafeteria was mixed.

There we were, in trouble.
He and I had been joking.
We spoke and laughed loudly.
We were punished every day.
No playground for us after lunch.

We walked around a pond.
We were two happy kids.
Going home from school,
We did not stop having fun.

We threw our backpacks in trees.
We wanted to eat the apples.
Sometimes we had to climb.
The backpacks got stuck.

We walked with the same friends.
We had big imaginations.
The countryside was our playfield.
What fun it was to go back and forth from school.

He Picked Me up From School

I was a student in Junior High School.
He was an apprentice.
I rode my bicycle every day.
He had a motorbike; one of our time.
Afterschool he came to pick me up.
He wanted to make sure that I would be fine.

We spoke on the road.
He always had something new to tell me.
We also spoke about our plans for the weekend.
He was my brother, my best friend.
We were two adolescents, loving each other.
We had values, respect and we were well educated.

When my brother picked me up from school,
I put my left arm on his right arm,
I did not have to pedal hard. He made my job easier.

I remember the curves where we had to slow down. We had a
long way to go, but time was never a problem.
Even after darkness fell, the road was fine.
I was protected because my brother picked me up.

He Was Going to Be a Priest

We grew up together as two happy kids.
The countryside was our playfield.
He wanted to be a priest.
We were very proud of him.

That morning, he asked me to not tell the widow.

He hid in the forest; did not want to go to the seminary.
It was after summer vacation.
He changed his mind about his Order.
We could not understand why.

He reappeared on time to go to the public school.

Mom was crying and walked us to the village.
I don't know what she was thinking.
We arrived at school.
It was the beginning of a new adventure for us.

He was not going to be a priest. We never discovered why.

Eighteen Years Old and the First Job

With my diploma I found a job right away.
I could have been an artist. I was good at playing theater.

I worked for the government; defense military.
The military wanted me to entertain the soldiers.
I did not know the world and I was afraid to travel.

I met a man who was married and we became best friends.
We had lunch together. People thought we were having an
affair.
I was interested in sports, social events and art.

My friend and I had our love in common.
We did not care what others thought.

I asked to meet his wife and children.
We all went to a restaurant and had a great time.
People stopped speaking about our friendship.

Then, he was relocated and I felt alone.

I met an engineer whom I liked very much.
He was a soldier.
We became girlfriend and boyfriend.
I was totally in love.
My life changed completely—love comes unexpectedly.
He was handsome; he had a Southern accent.
I was happy until one day his fiancée visited him.
What a disappointment it was in my life!

Once, at work, I had been crying in the computer room.
Suddenly I was kissed on the lips.
I did not get what happened for a while.
This young guy was touching my face.
He was speaking to me kindly.

I could not believe it.
I went back to my desk.
I thought of what happened.
I had to work, so ... I went on with my life.

No Psychological Help

My niece and I were the last customers.
I was eighteen years old. She was sixteen.
It was a wonderful Saturday.
I had my paycheck for the month.
I was in my bank to deposit it.

"Don't move," we heard.
We looked at the door.

No time to escape. I saw one man on each side.
The third one jumped over the counter.
"Nobody moves," he said.
He locked the employees in a room.
My niece and I were there, standing.

"May I sit?"
"Yes, you may," he replied

I felt as if I was going to faint.
Two of the men were masked.
The third was not. He took the money.
"Don't be worried. We will make love tonight."

It was at the time of a recession.
A lot of hold-ups happened.
Hostages were taken.

It could not be true that it was us in the bank.
People were looking from the outside.
For sure we would be hostages.
They, the gangsters, finally left.

The deputy sheriffs entered the bank.
They freed the employees.
They asked if we had been harmed.
We told them who we were.
We were to receive a call from them.

My niece and I were shocked.
We walked back home.
Why? We needed fresh air.

Forgiveness

You shall not kill:
Three gangsters were in my bank in France.
They could have killed me. They didn't.
I have a scar inside of me – anxiety.

You shall not judge:
One of them went to jail.
His cousin was wrongly accused.
I have a scar inside of me – anxiety.

You shall love your neighbor:
They terrified me. I am now scared of guns.
I don't trust people as I used to.
I have a scar inside of me – anxiety.

You shall forgive:
I have to make choices.
Right or wrong they were.
I have a scar inside of me – anxiety.

How can we forgive if we don't judge?
Forgiveness is about judgment.
My friend is right. They could have me killed.
I have a scar inside of me – anxiety.

I feel like I have to close my door.
I look behind me when walking.
I did not used to be that way.
They left me with a scar – anxiety.

I have a scar – anxiety.
Is that right or wrong?
Should I love them for it?
Should I forgive them?

Forgiveness is about experiences.
Forgiveness is about choices.
Forgiveness is about judgment.
Forgiveness is about letting go.

They left me with a scar – query?

We Received a Phone Call

My niece and I were minors.
21 year old was the legal age of adulthood.

We could not testify.
Identify, yes, so we went to the Sheriff's station.

We saw several pictures of men.
I don't remember if we had to try to recognize voices.

We were still in shock.
One picture attracted our eyes.
It was he, the one without the mask.

"It cannot be possible. He is in jail," we heard.
"The employees tell us the same."
He was the cousin of the man who was free.

I have been changed forever.
I became scared to be on a jury.
To this day I am still in shock.

It Was Meant To Be

He died and I was still working.
I thought of him every day.

A restaurant was near.
Reading a newspaper, I ate there.

There was laughter all the time.
A group of people was noisy, but polite.

A man came to me one day:
"Have you been in a plane before?" said he.

I answered, "Never; why?"

"My wife cannot come with us on a trip. Would you join us?"

It was as if I knew those people.
They were so lively in the restaurant.
Noisy maybe, but polite they were.

I accepted the invitation.
I knew that I could.

Here again, friendship. I had a paid hotel room for myself.

We went to visit the Chateaux de la Loire by plane one
weekend.
It was fantastic. We stopped at a wine cave.

We were lucky. The sky was clear and sunny.

It was my first time ever in a plane.
I was pampered.

Every weekend, I went to the airplane club.
I was adopted. I never paid for anything.

I ate with my new friends at the restaurant.
I became noisy, but polite.

I laughed a lot. They were good people.
Their wives were not jealous.

Memories

I was nineteen-years old.
I moved to Paris, 14ème Arrondissement.
I found a new and interesting job.

I became friendly with a boy my age.
I was accepted by his group of friends.
Every weekend we went to see a race.
It could have been cars or motorcycles.
He became my best friend.

One more time, people thought differently.
On a Monday morning my boss was quiet.
I went looking for my friend to say hello.

Up the stairs someone caught me; stopped me.
"He is not here. He had a car accident."
I went back to my desk. My boss stared at me.

"What happened?" I asked
"He died on a straight side of the road."
I could not believe it. I cried.

We were young and happy.
We had the same hobbies.
The next Wednesday I went to his funeral.

I've kept our memories.
In my heart he is, still.

Forgiveness

I had a living father only for eight years. He was loving and caring of his children. After he passed away our younger brother replaced him in our lives. He became our character reference. He was very fair, caring, loving. He did not have to tell us twice what we had to do. We understood the first time he spoke. We were obedient. We had good time, too, and our mother cherished those moments of laughter. It happened a lot in our lives. She was a character. She enjoyed joking. She made us laugh. She was a hard working woman on the farm.

My ex and I met at a young age. We married. He did not know how to deal with a woman. He had only brothers. He was all about work and advancement in the company he worked for. His father was his character reference. He was self-employed and rich. His wife, my ex-husband's mother, took care of the house, budget, and the education of their children. Their kids expected the same in their lives.

We decided that we would have our first child. I was still working. Loved it! My ex-in-laws pressured me to stop working and live their way. I was shy and at the same time strong. I decided I would give it a try.

When the baby was born our lives changed. I did not have time to realize what was happening around me. For three months the new born child did not allow me to sleep. She woke me up every two hours. I became a zombie. I slept on the sofa during the day with her on my breast and slept sitting still in bed during the night. I was disoriented and was crying alone.

At that time, there was no washing machine. There was no dryer nor diapers that you threw away. I spent my "free" time away from my baby doing this chore: washing clothes by hand. Cooking was necessary, as well as a daily routine of grocery shopping. Having a baby was pleasurable and at the same time, a mountain of new physical and psychological challenges in my life.

His routine did not change. He was studying for a promotion. I knew that I had married a competitive guy. I used to love working outside the home so I could understand this man. He was playing soccer, tennis and bridge. He still wanted to invite his friends over; to go to a restaurant or see a movie.

Once poor, I had become a woman of the upper-middle class. At the beginning of our marriage it was easy, but after the birth of our first child I was so tired that I did not balance the budget anymore. I was counting on my partner in life to help me, but that was not one of his priorities. I spent a lot of money for the baby. I started buying precooked appetizers from small shops and the most organic food. When we had friends over I cooked and bought the best wines for them. I spoiled myself in such a way to tell my ex-husband, *look at me. I exist.*

My ex-in-laws disapproved of my way of educating our child and taking care of their son. No, I was not going to wait for him to arrive at home and bring him his slippers or the newspaper! Yes, I was spending a lot of time with our baby. I had to. Yes, I loved her dearly. No, I was not a feminist, but we were living in a new era and women were asking for equality in the home. It should have been fair to share the education of our child in the evenings and during the weekends.

First Child

We visited them often.
We invited them often.
We decided to have a child.
A big change was coming.

I was working. I would have to stay home.
I was not sure that I was ready for it.
I enjoyed the work force.
My manager was good to me.

She was born. I stayed home.
Her father did not change his habits.
Work, tennis, soccer and no help at home.
I was by myself meeting a new life.

I did not have my driver's license.
He did the shopping on Saturday morning.
He became unhappy with that so I got my driver's license.
I was on my own.

I waited three months to visit my mom.
I could drive now and leave home.
He could do anything he wanted, and yet he became happy
with my independence.

I invited our friends over. I cooked.
We went to the Quartier Latin with our baby.
We chose the same big restaurant.
She was with us, happy.

I learned how to play tennis.
I found a babysitter. She was a neighbor.
She came to the tennis club with us.
She took care of our baby when we went to plays.

We bought a new apartment.
We moved out.
We stayed in touch with the babysitter.
She became the God Mother of our second child.

I Made my First Decision

He was playing soccer each Sunday morning.
Our daughter and I accompanied him.
It was a precious family time.

One Sunday he played next to my brother's house.
I made plans to visit him and his family.
My ex would drive us there and he would play soccer.

He wanted to come right home after the soccer game.
I agreed with that. He would take us with him.
After the match he would pick us up.

He left without us on Sunday morning.
That was a little bit unkind, I thought.

The transportation around Paris was wonderful.
I decided to visit my brother with my daughter.
I left a note for my ex-husband.
He did not have to worry.

Brother would be waiting for me at the train station.
Coming home, I would have to walk five minutes from the rail
station.
My plans were going to be okay.

After the soccer game my ex went home.
I don't know what he had been thinking.
He came to pick me up at my brother's house.

He was upset - let me know that I should never do that again.
Was that his ego speaking? Was that worry?
It was his ego. He was upset with me.

First time I made a decision on a Sunday morning.
He left without us. I had my day free.

I felt lonely during the week. He was studying for his job.
We did not speak. I waited for him until he went to bed.
I waited for our Sunday morning; to share some time together.

It was the first decision that I made without him.
He was upset – trying to scare me.
I was calm – did not speak a word.

Back at home he approached me too closely.
I was scared, but did not talk back.

She Was My World

I spent my days and nights with her.
The first three months were not easy.
She had a small appetite.
I breast-fed her every hour.

Both mother and child were exhausted.
I do remember falling asleep while seated on the bed.
She was there on my breast. She did not move.

The feeling of being mother was unbelievable.
It was hard because I also had to be a wife.
Cooking, washing, all at once.
I had no family near me. I did not feel lonely.

She lay down on my body when on the sofa.
I loved her. I cherished her. I would do anything for her.
She was my new born baby.

Her father was busy working.
I was bringing up this infant in the world.
It was great. It was a perfect world.
I don't regret a minute of it.

She was keeping me busy. I did not work; so I was telling the
people around us.
That's true. It was not work. It was love.
Love is a miracle. I thank God for it.
I thank her today for loving me back.
Together we are a team.

It Was a Village

I used to live in a big city, but we were a village; with
Schools, small shops, doctors, dentists, terrace cafes,
A church, library, gymnasium, etc.

We did our shopping every day. Everything was fresh.
Bones for our dogs awaited us at the butcher shop.
The people in our nine-story building were friendly.
We were as one family.

Living on the first story, I could watch the kids playing on the
playground.
Whenever they needed something they called my name.
After school, we adults spent some time outside with our
children.
We each had a pastry for a snack. The pastries were delicious.

The church, being poor, the priests were working.
We prepared the Mass for them and we taught the catechism.
The kids had the same activities and the parents were
carpooling.
The parents had the same activities and we met on a regular
basis.
My kids and I will always remember the good time we had in
the big city.

We were a village.

Twelve years in my First Marriage

We moved into a bigger apartment in 1975.
We had wanted a second child. I was pregnant.
I had a miscarriage.
Our first child was two year old.
She went to school – public day care.
It was called public school - it was free.
Paris was at 20 minutes by train.
We bought a membership to a private club.
We loved soccer and tennis.
As a volunteer, I taught tennis to the kids.
I became a volunteer secretary for the tennis club.

I was part of the PTA.
PTAs in France were different than those in America.
I had a membership through "The Federation Lagarde."
We made sure the government would listen to us.
We worked hard to give our kids a good education.
I went on each trip organized by the school: Paris, Versailles....

I became a volunteer for the Republican Party.
The elected officials at City Hall did not like our group.
I was very busy and yet I found time to play tennis every other
day.
We had a second child; a third one.
They kept me very busy. We hired a housekeeper.

I was always available for our kids after school.
They played outside for one hour each day.
We did the homework together.
My friends and I car-pooled to take the kids to their activities.
Television was banned for them except for one cartoon a day.
They took a bath. We had diner. I read them a story.
They went to bed. I went to meetings.

My children's father worked very late or studied at home for
his job.
He also played soccer on Sunday mornings. We watched him
play.
He played tennis on the week-ends. We were there too.
He played bridge during the week. We let him do it.

We were a group of friends; good friends - all Catholics. Not he.
We taught the catechism. We prepared a monthly mass for the kids.
We prepared the mass for the priests who were working.
I never said a word about my private life with my husband.
My two best friends knew about it.

We Established Ourselves

After the miscarriage we had to go on.
The doctor asked us to wait for a third pregnancy.
Our first child went to daycare.
It was governmental and free.
She was two years old.

I was not ready for that. He was not with us.
I thought that she was going to cry.
I prepared myself for not doing so in front of her.
I did not have to ask her to enter the classroom.
She went right away.

I spoke to the teacher. She asked me gently to leave.
I looked through the window.
Our daughter was playing. I could see her back.
Tears fell from my eyes.
I was relieved and at the same time, surprised.

I left and started my morning without our child.
I did nothing.
I drank a cup of café....
I read the newspapers. I could not concentrate.
I was waiting to pick up our child from school.

First Miscarriage

It was right before Christmas.
I was pregnant. I had a miscarriage.
I needed to go to the hospital.

My ex-husband did not seem to care.
He was not at the clinic for the birth of our child.
He was not at the clinic for the miscarriage.
It had been his choice.

He picked me up from the hospital.
We visited his parents with our child.
The traffic was heavy – ten hours of driving.

I had a headache throughout the holidays.
I spent my time in bed except during meals.
In fact I could not eat—not even once.

My headache became a migraine.
My mother-in-law visited once.
I cried. She asked me why.

I had a terrible migraine.
My ex-husband did not care.
I was too hurt to think about it.

It was the worse migraine of my life.
We went back home.
We did not visit my mom for New Year's Eve.
I had a migraine.

School Days

School started at 8:30am and went until 11:30am.
There was a recess between.
In the afternoon it was from 1:30pm to 4:30pm.

In day care, the children had a nap.
I picked up our daughter from school at 11:30am.
We went to the bakery before going home.

I bought a chocolate pastry and a baguette.
She did not eat well. She was like me when young.
Very thin she was. Just like me when young.

We ate. Often she had bread and butter.
Our family doctor seemed ok with that.
I cooked fish, steak, pork; everything I could.
She did not want to eat.

She was happy at school.
She loved to play with the other children.
She was a good listener. Her teacher loved her.

At 4:30 pm she ate her chocolate pastry.

We lived in an area with a lot of kids.
The apartments were built in a U shape.
There was a recreation area around them.
There was also a huge one in the center.

Men and women were outside after school.
The kids were playing altogether.
It was like living in a village.

At about 5:30pm we went back home.
Our daughter took a bath.
We spoke about her day.

At 6:00pm she was out of the bath.
We played games for an hour.
I cooked. She was in her bedroom.

When her father arrived, we ate.
At 8:00 pm he listened to the news.
At the same time, I was reading to our child.
He did not spend time with her.

New Year's Eve in France (Countryside)

One of my sisters, as well as her husband,
invited us to their home next to Normandy.
We dined on regional cuisine.
The seafood came from
a little village called Vannes,
where we bought fresh oysters.

I can still smell the oysters
that we consumed raw with lemon.
Each one of us ate a dozen.

We were about fifteen adults
and ten children, as well as babies.
The ambience in the kitchen was awesome.

Mussels, seafood, oysters;
Turkey cooked in the oven,
with a lot of fresh chestnuts.
The aroma of the cuisine
was overwhelming, along with
that of the bread on the table.
The plates of numerous cheeses;
lettuce and the buche glacée
complimented the end of the meal.

We all had long conversations.
We stayed at the table for three hours;
if not four.

Naturally, we had wine; red and white....
The kids had cider, water, juices, and milk.
We cleaned the tables.
We washed the dishes and then we danced;
the adults as well as the young children.
We loved the old songs of the 50s, 60s, 70s....

At midnight adults opened the bottles
of champagne for the New Year.
They drank from flutes.
We wished each other good health

for the new year coming,
and we continued to dance.

We all went to bed at three in the morning.
It was a precious time spent with the family.

Your Sisters Were in My Abdomen Too

I already had you, my child.
There was a baby in my abdomen.
I explained to you what was happening.

I did not know what to expect.
I loved you so much.
How could I love another child?

Was there place in my heart to love again?
Was that fair to you?
Those were the questions I asked myself.

She was here. I heard her crying.
I wanted to touch her.
She was beautiful.
I loved her right away.

I came back home with her.
Did not breastfed her; could not. I had the flu.
I was faint for several days.

Happily, I had a helper at home.
I was exhausted. I had to stay in bed.

After my recovery you wanted to feed her.
I sat you on the sofa; you held your sister.
You fed her. It was wonderful.

She became your opposite.
You were outgoing; she was calm.
She did not want me to leave her.
Where ever I went she had to be.

She played alone. She was quiet.
She did not want to go to day care.
You loved day care.

I brought her to the tennis court.
She followed me everywhere.
You were different. Still are.

I loved you both.

Today she wants to be a teacher.
When your younger sister was born it was easy.
You wanted to share your love with her.
You fed her. It was the continuity.
She loved school too.

My heart shared all the love I could possibly have.
We were a good team. Do you remember?
Certainly not; you were too young.

I am wondering what you were thinking.
Do you remember when you were babies?
I do. I still have my memories.

Playing Bridge in France in the Mid 70s

We were playing cards, an intellectual game.
I personally loved it for its quietness.
It was meditative, polite, and educational for me.
I felt as though I was learning. I enjoyed listening carefully.
This happened when with my friends.

They were playing cards, an intellectual game.
They were impolite, angry at each other.
It was a competition between couples.
They strayed from the rules. They did not care.

I started to learn with him.
We were married – I'd thought happily.
We should have been compatible.
But playing cards together was torture.

I decided that I would have it my way.
I spoke to the school principal.
The doors were opened for my friends and me.
We started our own club. We played Bridge.

I Was Not in Pain With Her

My first two daughters were born naturally.
I wanted another child but remembered the pain.
I found a doctor who respected and loved his wife.
He explained to me that things had changed.
He would take care of me and the baby.

I thought that I would not be a mother again.
It took one year before I conceived again.
She was there in my abdomen - then - unexpected.

I saw again the doctor.
He was right.
I gave birth without suffering.
She came into the world without trauma.

For my first daughter, birth was tricky.
The umbilical cord was around her neck.
I could not push as I had wanted too.
I was in pain for twelve hours.

My second daughter came out too fast.
She could have slipped from the hands of the doctor.
I was in pain for seven hours.

My third baby came without pain.
What a gift that was.

Was He an Angel?

Michael was his name.
His parents were devoted Catholics.

He had an older brother.
Michael was blond with curly hair.
He looked like an angel.

We left town for Christmas.
We were happy.
We came back joyous.
We were going to visit my mom.

My best friend came to visit.
She told me that Michael was dead.
I could not believe that fact.
I could not stop crying.

We had left town for the holidays.
I thought of this little angel all the time.
I could not see myself going to visit his parents.
I was ashamed to cry.

When we came back, school started.
I could still not speak to Michael's mother.

I finally met her after school one day.
She stopped me and told me, "I understand".
No she did not. I was ashamed of crying.

Who was I to cry more than the parents?
They were really believers.
I was not because I thought of the unfairness.
Michael was an angel.

She understood. We spoke for hours.
I cried even more.
She told me the first thing she did when she found Michael
dead
was to ring my door bell.

How did that happen?
I was not there. I was away, having fun.

I still cannot figure out why he left us so young.
He was a baby with blond and curly hair;
an angel that Michelangelo could have painted.

Baptism

When I was young, someone pushed me into the swimming
pool.
I have been afraid of the water since that day.

You were not. You liked it right away
in the bathtub; at the pool.

When you were baptized, you loved it.
The priest put water on your forehead.
You were a baby, you laughed.

Today you swim as a fish!

Medicine

My whole body was hurting, especially my back.
I decided to visit my mom's doctor.
He manipulated every part of me.
So softly, so gently, I did not feel any cracks.

I will always remember the feeling.
He let me go and told me:
"You will sleep for about two hours."
I slept three hours.

When I woke up my body was healed.
I had never met a doctor who manipulated me like this man
did.
He was young and working in the countryside.
He was gifted.

My Friend

We were neighbors with many kids around us.

We met through the love your two daughters had for mine.

I remember the summertime, when the heat wave hit France.

That year we became friends.

We played outside with our kids. Some other parents joined us
with theirs.

It was hide-and-seek parties for hours.
One of my daughters did not have teeth yet. You called her
Grandma.

You loved children and they loved you back.

I met your wife. She was as happy as you were.

You were in love and it showed to the rest of the world.

Your journey has been difficult.
You lost a child during the war time in a French colony.

We became inseparable; so I thought.

I moved to the United States.

You took care of the sale of my house in France.

The telephone was expensive. We did not have voice over
computer.

I dialed your phone number. Your wife answered.

You were at the hospital with a back problem.
Cancer was taking you away from us.

I called you there. I could not cry.

You were wondering....

You were wondering why you had to go still young.

I did not have the answer. I was losing my friend.

You left us with dignity.
I will always remember you.

An Unforgettable Moment

You now call from the right side.
Your other side is almost silent.
You listen from the right side.
The other side is quiet.

You had a beautiful room.
Our neighbor needed help.
She was sick with her grandson.
He was only four years old.

He went into your bedroom.
I was speaking with another neighbor.
A detailed groceries list I gave her.
I heard you screaming suddenly.

I could not find what happened.
After a while I realized.
I called the doctor right away.
You lost your hearing on the left side.

I was so proud of your bedroom. I included in it all the clinic
suggestions.

The doctors recommended that highly.

I had no idea of the danger: Q tips.

Dear You

Wherever you are,
I miss you; the two of you.

I was expecting you,
Yet I never met you.
You left my body too soon.

I was disappointed.
I was hurt.
It was not meant to be.

You are still in my mind
I hope to meet you again;
You are my babies.

I love you, I always will.

Did I Save Three Lives?

We saw them every day with their kids. They were always
smiling.
One morning someone rang our door bell. It was she.
She was crying; screaming; begging.
I listened.

We took the elevator; me, trying to understand her.
She was sobbing. We arrived at her entrance door.

Four gentlemen were there waiting for us.
They were deputy sheriffs.
I made a choice. I had to. Three lives were in danger.

I spoke to the man behind the door.
"Let me in please. I am not armed."

"I don't want them to come in."

"They will not. I promise."

"I want to die. I'll kill the kids first."

"You cannot do that. Please open the door."

The door opened and I entered the apartment.
The two kids were crying.
Their father had a gun pointed at me now.

"Don't do that now. Please look at your children."

"Everybody will die. I cannot live without her."

"I understand. Please put your gun away."

I faced him and asked if I could have something to drink.
He was surprised ... me, too.
He forgot about his gun for a few seconds.

I asked for permission to sit.
I was thinking of my children alone in our apartment.

I spoke and spoke and did not stop speaking.

I asked the kids to get dressed for school.
The father was crying now.
I asked him again to leave the gun on the table.
He did.
I hugged him.
I told him that now I would open the door.
I did.

The sheriffs came inside and took the gun away.
The mother asked me to testify. I said I would, but I would not
choose sides.
She agreed.

The sheriffs left.
I went to see my kids.
I brought the two other kids into our apartment.
And then we all went to school.

I called my doctor. He spoke to our neighbor.
The man spent all day in one of our bedrooms.
Did I save three lives?

Children Cooking

Watching, touching, smelling,
Rolling, curving, mashing,
Folding, sprinkling, blending,
Topping, stirring, adding....
Children are cooking fervently.

They make a mess—who cares?
It expands their imaginations.
They use their artistic vision;
Become part of the family tradition.
Clean up! Then fun begins.

Did Not Think I Could Do It

We had money to spend.
My children had everything they'd wished for.
They went to private schools.
We went for long, expensive vacations.
We had new cars.
Our house was almost paid off.

I needed to make a quick decision.

I would lose the material life.
Maybe my children would stay with their father.
I knew I would have to fight for my rights.

So, I made the decision.

I was ready to ask for the divorce.
He, my ex, asked for it first.
His witnesses put me down.
My witnesses told the truth.
My family was against me.
My mom was very hurt.

No one believed my cause.

I had only one friend, my brother.
Because of him I succeeded.
He gave me hope and never let me down.
One person can make a difference.
I won everything I needed.
My children were with me, safe and in good health.
I won. I am here to prove it.

I have been rewarded because of my perseverance.

I Made a Decision Because God Loves Women too

It was not easy. It was complicated; *surreal*.
The book of laws did not help me.
We were in the 20th Century.
We still lived under the rules of the Church.

Women's philosophers, Authors whose books I'd read from
during my first marriage
Helped me ***make a decision*** against violence in my home.

It was an expensive decision; I had to go back to work for it.
I never thought about putting money aside
To divorce my ex-husband, because I was also Catholic.
What my ex did was painful, outrageous, and disrespectful.

Exhausted and not knowing how it would go,
God guided me through the process.
One night, I asked Him to take me with Him.
The pain was unbearable.

He sent a woman to me in my sleep.
I woke up and stared at her.
All things around me were peaceful.
I could even see the full moon from my window.

From the peace I received that night
My heart went out to my children.
I had to do something for their happiness.
I never doubted the miracle.

The divorce went on and on. I lost assets; retirement.
From an easy material life, I had no choice but to go to work.
Educating my children was difficult; waking at 5:00am,
Coming back very late. I did it to protect them and myself.

Because of my appetite for intellectual growth,
I made a decision and I succeeded.
I fought the law; the Church.
God was on my side. He had a plan for me.
***I made a decision because I am a woman and God
loves me.***

I am a Gift in a Box with a Red Bow

I was strong. I wanted to die.
I laughed all the time. I lost myself in the space.
I wanted my children happy. I made them feel miserable.
I loved my husband. I made him unable to relieve my
pain. I wanted to be creative. My soul lost the light. I
wanted to be with people. I was lethargic.
I wanted to love. I hated.
I wanted to share. People were evasive. I loved my
brother. He left me too young. I wanted to go to Church. I
was rejected. I wanted peace. I fought – For what?

Life goes on. I am here. God loves me. Mary loves me.
They did not want me to quit. They have been my hope.
The songs in the Bible showed me the way.
I am here and I am a gift because one day I will be able to
share in a decent way how women, men and children can
find a way out of unbearable circumstances.

I should not have been born. God had a plan for me.
I am His gift.

I deserve a red bow – red being the gift of life – the blood
of Jesus Christ.
I am a gift and I am getting out of my box.
Maybe that's why I love my hair red.

An Unforgettable Character

In my youth I remember that the Woman inspired me. I did not think of God. She was the one who said yes without understanding really what the consequences would be. She said yes because she already had the spirit in her. I have followed her life for years. I fell in love with the Woman who was so inspirational to the people in my native country. We did not read the Bible. We went to catechism. She was the story behind the scene. She was the child, the woman, the wife, the friendship.

I also believe that she appeared numerous times to faithful children or saints. Was she then the woman I saw in my bedroom when I was so desperate? Why did she appear to me when I asked God to take me to a better place? I know: half-sleep, the mind playing a game, the subconscious, my own picture. I agree. I cannot be sure. I just feel that she could have been real and thus what does it mean? I remember her. I remember the ultimate peace around me. I was not floating, not on drugs not on medication. In the early 1980s, reading a lot, I knew what was going on in the lives of women and children. We were millionaires. I spent money as it came in because it was my way out of a miserable marriage. It was spent mostly on the children for them to feel secure outside the home. No excuse. I spent it and it did not go through my mind that I should put some aside for a divorce. In fact I rejected his money.

I finally was running from being battered and being insulted. No way out; or so I thought. I was not thinking about *if* or *what*. I was clearly advancing in my life. I knew my children needed me. They let the judge know that. With the information she had, they chose to follow my path. I earned respect. I started to work outside the home. The judge decided I was still young so I could do it. She was right. I did not care for my retirement. I cared for my kids. I did not care for the money. I was driven by the challenge. I could not despair. I was now in charge of my children's lives as well as my own. I will always remember: I wanted to help others when my children were on their own. I wanted to be close to God. Thanks to God for the woman I saw that night. In some ways she was me and I was her. Together we were united. My commitment to her was to help her through my actions. Whatever her name is, she remains a mystery to me. Of all that I know, she does not look like me, even if she and I seem to be of the same character. Now that I have been able to speak more clearly about her, I know I am challenged. I am not scared. I feel peaceful. I want to go on with my life thinking, writing, and acting as an advocate for people who are less fortunate than I. It starts with me. That's certainly why she visited me and that's certainly what she wants of me. We are unified. Who can tell me who is who?

An Unforgettable Character

I recall her long, black, straight hair with bangs.
Her eyes were dark-brown; enigmatic, profound.
She was tall and motherly.
Her gown was white and made of cotton.

I could see flowers as embroidery.
Staring at me, mysterious, she was silent.
She brought with her the ultimate peace.
If Heaven is that peace-loving it's extraordinary.

I knew that if I closed my eyes I would lose the woman. I did
close my eyes.
She became my helper then.
We won a trial on earth together.

She left me with questions: How did she know
how much I could endure?
She has brought me eternal peace: what was her goal by
visiting me that night?

I embraced her because she was a messenger.
Knowing what I know, she came for us.
Can you see her, feel her?

A New Faith

When I was young I went to church regularly.
Once married, I stopped going.
I had good values, but never read the Bible.
Praising God, I sang songs of love.
I taught catechism and was happy with the children.
When I visited my mom, once a week her priest was there.
She received communion at her home.
The priest was devoted to the community.
People could go to the presbyter to play, "La Pétanque"
He also appointed a room where people could meet to
celebrate.
He was a remarkable man.

The priest was soft spoken, amiable, caring.
With him in my mom's life, I felt comfortable to speak about
God.
I sent him letters from America to thank him.
This priest has been a delight in my life.
I think I have found the same kind of person here.
He had surgery not too long ago.
I will certainly restore my faith in speaking with him.

The Stranger

It was late. I came home from work.
No more bus. No more train.
I was driving my car.

I stopped by a stranger.
I drove him home with me.
I prepared a meal for both of us.
We then spoke.

He had a dream. I had one too.
It was a tree house.
He drew one on a cover of a book.
We were united.

I asked him if I could drive him home.
His answer was soft; *no, I will be fine*.
Who was this stranger in the street?

I never saw him again.
He is still in my mind.

First Day

I see him walking
I know at first sight
I will be loved.

He opens his lips
I hear his beauty
Universal love.

We speak for a while
He returns to work
I stay at my desk.

I don't think further.
I saw him in my dream;
on a peaceful night.

God sent him to me
When looking for him
Destiny awaits.

I'm waiting now
For the adventure.
It's the beginning.

He Had a Near Death Experience

Here he was with a child's illness.
His fever was very high.

He travelled in time.
His mind went far away.

The light attracted him.
He refused to enter it.

He came back to meet with me.
He and I are now inseparable.

Letting Go of the Children

When he was not going to come back I fell very depressed.
We had shared weekends with the kids. We were family.

I could not afford to pay the rent by myself.
This time I would not make it.

Working with three kids was a big task.
I missed him. I cried every day.

We needed each other. We were so in love.
I did not know what to do.

I stayed focused at work.
I stayed focused at home.

Having not paid my rent, I did not know where to stay.
I did not want to scare the children.

I needed to think.
I had to make a decision.

I would call the social services.
My kids and I would be separated.
I could not go on with my responsibilities.

A friend of us offered us a bedroom in his small house.
We were safe once again.

Back Into the Business World

Returning from a foreign country, we bought a house.
My friends had moved out of their apartment, too.

I did not recognize the neighbors and the area was no longer
safe.
We moved. My ex-husband was still in America.

Our children went to an international school.
I looked for a job, although I did not have the experience.

I became a temporary employee, learning new software every
three months.
I could have been hired anywhere, but the salary was better as
a temporary. I also had benefits. I needed money for the
divorce—a lot of money.

My ex-husband came back to France. He knew what I was
going to do, but he did not believe that I could do it.

He thought that the material life was everything to me.
One day, at work, I was given the divorce papers.
It was a decision from him that pushed me to tenacity.

I would give my arguments to the judge.
I would hire the best lawyer in France for women and children.
I did—I was strong—knew what I was doing. It was for a cause.

The judge settled the divorce right away.
I needed to fight for full custody of our children.
It took more time—four long years of agony.

Meanwhile I met a man who owned a restaurant.
I worked for him from 10:00am to 1:00 am.
I loved that job but a voice told me to quit.

I went back into the workforce as a temporary.
The agency needed someone like me to save a contract.
It was an American company.

I accepted the job for only one month.
I had to work all over Paris.

I lived in the west. The workplace was in the east.
The travel time was too long.

Because of the time difference between France and America
I had to start early and finish late.
My bus left at five o'clock in the morning and returned at nine
o'clock in the evening.

The feeling I had for the restaurant I did not have for this new
job.
It was a field I had never worked in: construction.

I learned as I went and I was happy. I decided to stay for good.
The company hired me. I was spending my time with artists.

For the first time I really enjoyed working for and with others.
It had been the best experience I'd had in France as a single
mother.

My nephew, who had been working in Paris, was living rent
free in the house.
He took care of my children. I started to be me again.

I had parties for the kids almost once a month.
I'd rather to do that than have them go to other people's
houses.
The parents trusted me and I knew what the children were
doing.

Working with the World

You and I were now boyfriend and girlfriend.
Everyone knew of our love story.
We were invited to parties, dinners.

My children were with us.
Being a single mom was not easy.
I needed to take care of my youngest.
She stayed with me at work for Easter Holidays.

Our manager did not like it.
Maybe he did not approve our love story.
He asked me not to work for you anymore.
He was still my manager but in another department.

Some people don't have their hearts in the right place.
I was a hard worker and I should have been understood.
I was finally laid off from the engineering department.
Not because I was not professional; because of you, her and
me.

Happily a manager needed an assistant.
He offered me the job.
His wife and I became friends.
My child was welcome at the office.

When We Met

When we met, we spoke for hours.
There was a flow of words between us.
Often, I did not understand them.
You explained to me with great patience.

The pleasure was incommensurable.
Between us were interpretations. We needed to search
incessantly.
We, today, understand each other.

You are a Gift to Me

I was reading a book.
Something black attracted my eyes.
It was your trench coat.

My sandwich was on my desk.
I heard, "Would you help me?"
Surprised, I looked at you.

"Naturally, what do you need?"
It was a letter to be typed.
Surprisingly, it contained the word *divorce*.

I was divorced, too.
We spoke about the lawyers;
all of the money we spent.

We began a serious conversation.
Then you left me to go to work.
I could see your desk; the people visiting you.

You were a consultant then and I, a secretary.
We became interested in each other.
We had lunch with the team.

You lived at the Grand Hotel; an expensive place.
You invited me to visit you there.

I bought a new outfit at the Gare Saint Lazare.
I walked to the hotel. I was not sure who you were.

I walked back and forth in the main street.
I felt confused. Do I go? Do I ride the metro?

I finally asked for the number of your room.
I knocked at the door. You opened it.
You thanked me for coming.

We spoke for hours. We enjoyed it.
We even had dinner inside the hotel.

You were a gentleman and very bright.
You walked me to the metro station.

I returned home, liberated.
I found that day, one man who respected a woman.
No sexual approach—what a discovery!

It has been the beginning of our story.
Today, I would like to thank you.

My children liked you right away.
You invited us to visit places.

You made my mom laugh.
You made my brother laugh.

You must be a special person.
You are a gift to me.
I love you.

You Were Going To Come Back

We were officially together. Everyone knew about it.
You left, to return in three weeks.

That was what your contract should have read.
Three months in France; three weeks in America.
The company decided that small consultants
would no longer be hired.

You were not coming back.
I moved from the west of Paris to the east.
You were going to move with us.
You were not going to come back.

We made the decision to marry.
We had to wait at least three weeks.
Fax, phone calls, visits to the City hall - on my side.
School registration, medical visit, faxes – on your side.
Immigration papers too.

You thought of working in France.
You did not speak French. You were busy working.
The best would be for us to move with you.

Everything was finally done. We married.
We needed now to take care of the immigration.
My ex did not want the children to go.

We all ate together at my brother's house.
He met with you—we had a lengthy conversation.

He knew where the children would go to school.
He knew that we were married.
He did not want the children to leave.

I had to sign the papers for the sale of the house.
He and I went to the City Hall the next morning.
I asked him to sign the paper to allow me to leave.
I signed the paper for the sale of the house then.

I was married, and he had someone in his life, too.

The Lioness

She was roaring at him.
He walked around her.

She was appealing to him.
He was not sure.
She was calling him.
He approached her.

He did not know....
she was roaring at him.
Together they met.

Could Not Fight Anymore, or So I Thought

You were not coming back.
I could not afford to pay my rent, my utilities.

I felt as if God had abandoned me.
Why this new test?

Exhausted, I could not go on with them;
them being my children.

They were sharing my life.
The oldest was in a private school.

What could I offer them?
My heart was bleeding.

I saw only one way.
I had to separate myself from them.

I could not do that.
Their father would have asked for them.

I would have to explain why I did not want that to happen.

Would he have them with him?
It was not agreeable.

We moved into a friend's home.
We were safe again.

An Unforgettable Moment

We were lovers for the first time.
I gave you my body, my mind.
We were one; each other.
My soul, I shared with you.

I suddenly saw an empty field.
A daisy - *two daisies* were blossoming.
The field became white and yellow.
The daisies stopped growing.

My body was laying down on them.
My body was floating above them.
The images stopped.
I was quiet, happy, in love.

My lover, I knew, I would marry.

My Love

After our first meeting at the Grand Hotel
You picked up my kids and me during the weekend.

You invited us to the restaurant.
We visited zoos and went to different places.

You loved to travel and discover Europe.
We shared our feelings about it.

We could speak about work.
We enjoyed the company who hired us.

I remember one time I was exhausted.
We had planned an evening at the restaurant.

We were waiting for our friends.
I ate appetizers; drank two glasses of wine.

You found me sleeping on your shoulder.
You did not know what to do.

You brought me to your hotel room.
I still do not remember a thing.
I was too exhausted.

You took off my shoes.
You put the blanket on me.

I woke up in the morning, revitalized.
I slept as an angel that night.

I knew that nothing had happened.
You were a gentleman. Still are.

We had a long conversation, as usual.
You were very interesting to listen to.

I started to see you as a loving man.
You drove me back home.
My children were happy to see us.
You spent the afternoon with us.
Our day was delightful.

Thank you, my love, for your soul.

An Immigrant's Life in the USA

I am a naturalized citizen. When I came to the USA 21 years ago, I did not speak English.

We moved to Burbank, California, where even doing my grocery shopping was difficult. To buy a specific cut of meat, I went to the grocery stores with the translation on a piece of paper from the dictionary. That's only one example.

Calling people over the telephone was a tremendous effort. My accent was so strong that nobody understood me.

My children went to a bilingual school and became fluent in English very quickly. My husband was at work, my kids at school. I was on my own. I read newspapers, magazines, and books. I tried to speak English with our neighbors. In the evening, when everybody was at home and around the dinner table, we spoke Franco-American. My husband and kids were my teachers. This went on for a year before we moved to Santa Clarita, California.

My husband and I created our own company at home. When he went to a meeting I prayed the phone would not ring. I could not understand people's names. The alphabet may have been the same, but the spelling of words was different. If we were invited to people's homes, I did not speak. . I think of the oldest generations of immigrants and what they had to go through with a new language, new culture, etc. Did they, too, cry when alone? They wanted the best for their children by making them learn the English language. It is so beautiful to write, read and speak a foreign language fluently. This is one of my dreams. I hope that I will achieve it in the USA.

Speaking a Second Language

"You should speak English," I was told.
I had been told that for numerous years.
When said so often it makes one shy.
I did not want to speak at all.

Happily my husband was nice.
He joked a lot teaching me his language.
He made up new words to make me laugh.
I never knew if he was telling me the truth.
It was a game between him and me.

The children smiled at us often.
"It was not funny," I was saying.
"It is," he was answering.
Between him and me it became a habit.

It was really funny to learn that way.
I learned to speak making mistakes.
He was laughing at them.
I taught myself to be less shy.

He was happy with my progress.
He asked me to not pay attention.
People don't always understand.
We still make up our own words.
We laugh when it happens.

My Creation

We were married. I did not have a job.
We were happy. I wanted to work.
We both needed a job.

We decided to build our own company.
He said that I would be the vice-president.
I took the title seriously.

He would create the documents.
I would format them in the computer.
The main problem was my inexperience.
In France we already used Windows.
Here, not.

"DOS" operating system would be my challenge.
We bought two big books.
How would I be able to understand them?
Their language was technical.

I broke my personal barriers.
I became somewhat a designer.
The results on the paper were quite professional.
I felt that I could finally use my title.
It became my creation.

Custody of the Children

We were in America. Hadn't heard from my lawyer.
I called the judge. My file was
archived.
I explained the why all over again.

His lawyer stated that I had left with a friend of mine.
One more lie coming from his side.
The judge did not believe him.
She gave me full custody of the children.

Administratively, the fight was over.
The fight continued as he called the children.
He was writing to them.
He blackmailed me with Interpol.

The law was on my side - the Consul was aware.
We could now start our new life.

My Furniture

My brother and some friends helped me move.
My furniture, bought with credit, was new.
We could not have it right away in the USA.

One of my friends, a mover, would take care of it.
The white sofa made in Italian leather diffused some pink.
The dining room was modern, made of light.

When the time came to have it here, I asked for my things.
I was sent clothes, books and papers.
The furniture was missing.

He, my friend, used it at his home.
With the French law, I could not be helped.
I lost the furniture that I had fallen in love with.

I was hurt; in disarray.
Who would have believed a friend doing such a thing?

Crisis

After my furniture was stolen, I did not feel the same.
One day I visited my husband at his office.
I had to go up a hill to return home.
Even my daughter had a hard time walking.
I was telling myself it would be easy.
I did not feel my body anymore.
It was as if I did not have one.
I saw something grey around my head.
I could breathe. I could run.
I could even dance.
The hill became friendly.
Was that power over mind?
This feeling I will have forever.

Crisis

I wondered about the world.
I should not have trusted my friend.
My brother would have kept it safe.
He would have sent me my furniture.

I loved my books, photographs, clothes.
I did not know what to make of it.
How to trust again?

I had a fever.
I decided to unpack.
I donated a lot of books to a college.
The rest I threw away; the trash was full.
I became depressed.

Crisis

He was suffering from his back.
Mom asked me to visit him.
I thought I was prepared.
When I saw him, we both knew.
I went to the kitchen to cry.

My little brother was dying.
My brother was leaving me.
He was not even fifty years old.
This time would be the last.
We joked. We spoke. We never cried.

Our mom was very hurt.
She became very sick.
I kissed them both good-bye.
It was the last time.

I could not go to the funerals.
I would not have come home
France was my mom, my brother.

My place was here, in the USA.
My husband awaited me.
My children and grandchild awaited me.
To survive, I needed all of them.

Crisis

After their deaths the world changed around me.
My best friends were gone.
I was left isolated.

I promised myself I would make it.
I would concentrate on my adopted country.

I bought books in English.
I bought new American clothes.
I took an oath to my adopted country.
I became American in my heart.

The hurt became sorrow.
I missed my mom, my brother.
They left me empty.
How would I survive their deaths?
I fell alone just thinking about it.

It would have been helpful to speak.
Things from my past, again I cleaned.
I wanted to be reminded of nothing.
The present was still too hurtful.
For the first time I had no future.
The depression aggravated.

Forty Years Passed

You became the pillar of the family.
How did that happen?
I was sick.
You comforted me.
I was not going to make it.
You were strong for me.
I no longer had courage.
You helped me go on.
You are my oldest daughter.
Thank you for your strength.

Crossroads

Working in our home has been, is still, a necessity.
It, at the same time, secludes me from the world.

I have friends in you now and I share my life with you.

Church was difficult to attend.
Divorced and married again, I felt rejected.
I do go now and God is in my heart.

One of our children had a difficult time.
I lost my joy for life. We had to go through a bad time.
She is fine now and I can breathe better.

I've lost most of the people I've loved the most.
My father-in-law passed away last week.
I want to help my husband to go through his grief.

I would like to thank you all of you who share your writing.
I have hope that I will write a book one day.
If it is not for me it will be for a cause.

I will fight my depression, for I know that I am loved.
I owe that to my husband, children and grandchildren.
I owe my life to them.

My Doctor

You speak my native language.
The why; the how you understand.

When necessary you decline medication.
Meditation is in your vocabulary.

Thoughts you welcome.
Conversations you try to have.

You are a wonderful doctor.
I am happy to have met you.

Buff Charlemagne

You were a Gift to the family

I needed a friend and I found you.
You were in a small cage.
You appeared to be lonely-sad.
I was attracted to you.
Your price was one hundred dollars.
I needed someone to talk to and to love.
I saw you ... I watched you.
I loved your beige and white color.
You did not look to be a pedigree.
I called my husband immediately. I bought you.
I returned home with you and we played for hours.
You became our baby.
You ran inside our home and slid on the tile.
You did not like the outdoors.
We had so much fun with you!
The tennis ball was your favorite game.
You jumped back and forth on the sofa to retrieve it.
You grew up-you were very protective.
What a joy to be next to you!
Charlemagne was your French name.
Buff was your American one.
You understood the Franco-American languages.
You were buff.
You impressed people—it was funny.
No one was as gentle as you were.
We had you with us for 7 years.
It was too early when you left us.
You had a prostate cancer.
You had surgery, but it was too late.
We kept our sofa to remember the good times.
Thank you for your love.
We will never forget you, Buff.
You were a gift to the family.

In The Year 1994

4:30am: I was in a deep sleep. Surprised by a noise, I woke up. It did not bother me at first. The walls were red. The windows were red. *We were attacked,* I was thinking. I was unable to react right away. Suddenly, the noise was tremendous. I got up quickly, running into the bedrooms of our children. I asked them to go downstairs with me. My husband was upstairs, screaming. We could sense how worried he was. "Where are you?""Here," I said. From downstairs we could not see the red sky. We waited for my husband to join us under the stairs. He arrived and turned the light on. "You don't have your slippers on."I was wondering what was wrong. It did not take long to see and understand what the problem was. The picture frames on the wall were on the floor, broken. We could see pieces of glass everywhere. *We have no shoes on,* I told myself. I was now worried for the children. I went upstairs and came back downstairs with their slippers as well as my own. I was in shock. I told my husband, "We have been attacked. Have you seen the sky?"He answered, "It is an earthquake."I felt earthquakes maybe twice before. They did not disturb me. In fact, when we moved into our home, the same night we had one. It was a 3.2 magnitude. I barely felt it. Now I was confused.

We went to the dining room and living room. All of the shelves from our library were upside down. The books were on the floor. We walked into the kitchen. Its floor was slippery. The bottles of salad dressing, the cans, etc. ... from the pantry, were all mixed together, broken on the floor. The tile was not pink anymore but yellow, white, red and brown. The doors of the cabinets were open and the dishes were on the floor. In the family room, the picture frames were broken. Only the statues from Mary and Jesus Christ were fine. What a coincidence I was thinking! They were on the fireplace. The bricks did not break, but moved about one inch. We turned the radio on. Yes, it had been an earthquake. Why the red sky? We looked at the valley below our home. Some houses and a transformer were on fire. Because we had our business at home, we had three phone lines. One was working. We went outside. We met with our neighbors. We spoke. I was scared now. They were speaking about aftershocks. I had no idea what that was. The adults drank café; the kids had hot chocolate or juices. Our neighbors were worried because they could not call their relatives. We invited them over to our house to use our telephone. Meanwhile, my husband cleaned the kitchen floor. No school that day. We all stayed outside until late in the evening. The City did an excellent job at providing the necessary resources for emergencies. It was very efficient. Our valley was closed off and isolated from the other valley. A bridge had been broken. The National Guard helped us with water, etc. The Red Cross was set up in the school gymnasiums and associations were helping in the parks. I could not stay home. I drove around the city with the kids to help as much as we could. I did not want to call my family in France. One morning I received a phone call from my young brother. The effects of the earthquake were on T.V. overseas. I had no idea. I did not want to tell my relatives that I was very scared. I thought I would tell them, "I want to move back to France."

The conversation was short but helpful. I think I am still in shock. I am not prepared for another earthquake of magnitude 7.2. This one had been centered in nearby Northridge.

Growing Older

Projects don't follow through.
Recession reminds us of it.
Work is still a necessity.
Growing older is not easy.

Health care is the empire.
For us it is a real burden.
We have to pay for; into it.
Growing older is not easy.

Clothing is less a bargain.
If made in China not a big deal.
Korea, India, Africa all pay less.
Growing older is not easy.

Groceries have become less affordable.
Gasoline adds to their expense.
The minimum wage is low.
Growing older is not easy.

This Holiday I Will Look at Them

It used not to be the most beautiful time of the year.
I had no plans, no dreams, nor wishes for the holidays.

I was living secluded from the world.
I was ashamed to be ill. I could not forgive myself.

So strong, so confident and nevertheless so fragile;
I hid myself in my home. Work was the excuse.

I could have continued to be a volunteer; but did not do
it.
I was wondering what people would have thought.

I became ill not because of my past but the present.
I could not bear this new learning in my life;
could not understand how it had happened so fast.

I was going to lose my child. It could not have been true.
I was having a nightmare.
They were all my children.
I could have lost one of them; nothing that I could have
done.

I was praying. I was crying. I wanted to scream ...from the
bottoms of my lungs.

I was going to lose my child. She wanted to leave us.
There was no way that I could see people and speak about
it.

I was alone in my home; I did not want to have
conversations.
I had a terrible time, but for my child it was worse.

I had to not judge, but to understand; not be detrimental
to my child.
I had to accept—survive—not quit loving my child.

I had to try to be her—watching over her—breathe with my child.
What a nightmare it has been, but today she is safe.
This year she sparkles.

This year I see the light in her eyes, so even if I have an illness
I will enjoy the holidays. My child is alive and me with her.

This year, I will be at my best for the husband I love.
I will laugh from the conversations between our kids and their husbands.

This year, I will enjoy the happiness in the eyes of our grandkids.
This holiday, I will look at all of them and feel blessed.

How Does That Happen So Fast?

Our first child: she hides behind the curtain. Suddenly I hear, "Can you see me?" I see her face.... It is our first hide-and-seek together. She likes to watch gymnastics on T.V. She wants to practice that sport. I register her in a club of very young athletes. She is scared, but she practices everything the coach asks her to do. She is now tired and wants to sleep. Good night little girl....

Our second child: she has a small water gun in her hands. She tries to point it at us. The direction of the gun is not the right one. Here she is with her face wet!

She is only two years old. She has a small racket in her right hand and a very soft ball in her left hand. She plays on the wall of the tennis club. It's amazing to see her running and so patient for hours.

Our third child: she is loved by the neighbors. The teenagers fight over her. They want to take her with them to the bakery. She is spoiled, does not cry, but smiles.

She is five years old. Between her and the water there are three meters. She learns to dive. The height scares her. Is she going to jump? She does. She is proud of herself; we are too.

Here we are at the ceramic club. Christmas approaches. All of us make our own ornaments. What a delight for me to watch them have fun! Naturally they pick on each other sometimes. Today they are grown up; have children of their own.

How does that happen so fast?

The Middle Child

It was not easy to fit in with an out-going sister.
Your silence equalized your world.
You were singing your own songs.
You were dancing to your own music.

Your friends were just like you.
You were all Independent and needy.
Calling for me was your free time.
Touching me was your safety.

You are grown up, a future teacher.
Speaking to others is your freedom.
Your words you are now revealing.
You are not shy anymore.

Quiet

Calm and quiet, you grew up as a flower.
Close to him and me - you were looking for us.
You wanted us to carry you in this world.
You paid attention to our words.

Friends and peers mixed in one you found.
I could feel your anxiety in being so advanced.
You were smaller, younger; it was difficult.
You wanted to identify yourself.

They called you *Little Sister;* they protected you.
I was happy for you; you were not.
You dreamed. You wished you were taller.
Your qualification was troubling your life.

I want to let you know you are grand.
Your heart is made of jewels.
You are well suited for the world.
I love you forever, my quiet child.

Christmas 2011

They were all speaking.
They were all laughing.
Happiness was all around me.

I was listening and smiling.
I barely remember that time.
I missed my Mom so much.

This year was different.
I was Mom. I was special.
I was Grandma. I was special.

I saw myself that way for them.
I realized that I was their gift.
They love me so much.

This year I thought of my Mom.
It did not make me cry.
I was the one I should have been for years;
A wife, a mother and a grandmother.

My eyes were wide open; as well as my heart.
I love them all so much!

She Was Mom

How blessed I have been to have been loved without exception.
She was the widow, the woman whom I respected.

I was taller than she, a petite woman.
Her heart was filled with love and compassion.

I received blessings almost all of my life from her.
She did not have to explain, her eyes spoke for her.

I listened to her carefully because she was wise.
She had the gift of acceptance and knew how to joke.

I loved her and no one could hurt her. I protected her.
She taught me lessons of life by sharing her life. Not enough.

I would like to have known this woman better and to
remember.
She was a gracious, intelligent, hard working woman.

I was spoiled. She did not want my help.

She enjoyed the company of my kids and my visits.
I gracefully spent a lot of time with her. Not enough.

She was my Mom and how much she had loved me.
I now am a mom and I try to pass that love on to my heirs.

My Mother

A voice told me
to love and respect her.

Her hair was white,
and her heart was purple.

She gave me life.
She held me first.

She taught me my first smile.
She woke up during the nights.

She healed me then.
She wanted the pain for her.

She used her hands to heal me.
She passed away. I felt lost.

I will forever love my mother,
for she gave me the tools to carry on.

I will persevere in the adversity of life
because she was an inspirational woman.

Mom

Petite; her eyes were dark brown.
She was elderly with white hair.
Her skin, bronze, was beautiful.
She liked blue and white clothes.

Quiet, mellow; she spoke softly.
She knew what smiling meant.
Laughing was her joy.

After her daily duties she sat.
It was around 4:30pm.
I sat on the floor next to her.

She caressed my hair magically.
We then spoke as two adults.
It was an enchanted time.

She passed that tradition on to me.
I still do the same with my children.
I miss the touch of my mom.

Our Parents

Our parents are the capital city of our hearts.
They are as the most wonderful city in the world.
They gleam in the daytime and at night,
teaching us right and wrong,
and they love us every day.

Our parents, with excellent qualities,
reveal to us the righteous, the accurate
and teach it always.
Their jurisdiction is without borders.
They do not quit their jobs; *ever.*

Our parents are the capital city of our hearts.
And now that we live with their inspiration,
hoping that we will succeed as they did--we will teach their
values to our own children.

Convalescent Home

His wife died.
His children moved out of State.
With inspiration he wrote.
He wrote poems about God.

She scared me.
Her hands were strong.
She had a stroke.
I learned how to dry her lips.

She was funny.
She wore rollers all day long.
She put nail polish on a daily basis.
She always told stories about stars.

She never smiled.
She was angry all the time.
We did not know what to expect.
We let her alone most of the time.

She was suffering.
She was in excruciating pain.
Tears fell from her eyes.
She spoke softly. We could not hear her.

These are some of the people I have known.
These are some of the people I have loved.

Love Song

How handsome you are, my love.
Your blue eyes resemble the sea.
Your lips make me thirsty.
Why is that we love to kiss?

You and I are lovers.
I love your touch.
You are my strength.
I desire you in my heart.
Why I did not meet you sooner?

We explore our world with long conversations.
They are beneficial to our marriage.
We laugh, we joke, and we're serious.
We entertain our relationship.
Why is it so fruitful for our love?

We are dedicated to each other.
We have made a promise for life.
We nurture the seed of our wedding.
It has been twenty one years. Why do you and I grow like a
plant?

I will always love you.
You are my husband.
My other half I found in you.
I know why.
You and I are an inspiration for our children.

Love Song

When I met you, I had already seen you before. I saw you in a
vision.
You appeared to me during the night.
I did not recognize you right away.
Today I do, because you are the one.
It was written somehow.
What a coincidence.

You were a good driver.
You never got lost.
But that evening you lost your way.
Your car passed my house.
No direction, you were looking for another way.
We met then, unexpectedly.
It was as a magical world.

Words flowed constantly between us.
They were as a calm river.
Built of soft current they sounded peaceful.
They entertained the mind.
They fed the spirit.
They never let us down.
What a great experience it was and still is.

Love Song

My love, you are a fountain of hope.
Your words, a river of life, make me dream.
My love, you are a fountain of wisdom.
You are as the wind; transparent.

The earth seems so beautiful with you around me.
The sky is so peaceful when I am on your side.
The stars are exquisite with you during the night.
You are my universe, the one with the spirit.

Paradise is closer when I dance with you.
I share with you happiness, memories.
Together we rearrange the world around us.
We show our children that love is universal.

Love Song

I cannot resist thinking about you.
Your skin is as warm as a book.
With your lips I can open it. Your eyes are the lines.

The ink is wet and salty.
It comes from your tears.
It becomes dry then.
The thought has passed.

A smile on your mouth is the feeling.
I look at you. You are in another world.
What emotion is going through your mind?
You become serious; what a change.

Your face is an open book.
I can read it every day.
You are my consciousness.
You are an open book.

Love Song

Your language is my garden.
It blossoms in my spirit every day.
It enriches my mind when not expected.
It is the present and the past.

A book of words my garden is.
Fidelity, trust, love is its path.
It blossoms unconditionally.
It is the spiritual dictionary.

My garden is your language.
Your lips are made of buds.
They open when read.
Their place is universal.

Love Song

Whenever you move, I move.
Whenever you speak, I speak.
You approach me silently.
I approach you quietly.
You touch me, inside of me.
I let you feel my desire.
Sometimes it is your eyes.
Sometimes it is my lips.
We share the understanding.
You and I are made for each other.

Love Song

I believe we still have a long life together.
Your curiosity will always be the same.
Your knowledge you will bring to others.
Your world you will accomplish with me.
Your thirst for good news you will pass on to me.
I want to learn from your words.
I want to benefit from them.
I enjoy learning on a daily basis.
Why is that I love the sound of your voice?
It pleases my ears; goes thru my fingertips.
Words then move freely on the keyboard.
I lose time in space.
Your words are music with a magical plan.
You don't want to hurt me or harm me.
I am finally at peace with you by my side.
Sorrow is far behind me.

I am not scared; you pay attention to who I am.
Your voice is quiet, soft; a lake with no current.
I learn how to listen patiently; serene I am.
Thank you for this moment.

Love Song

It is a new day.
I am waking up.
My mind is on you.
I am settled.
The words flow already.
I feel my heart.
The birds are singing.
I see the valley.
What a beautiful morning it is.

Love Song

He made a promise that day.
He said he would love for me forever.
He fulfilled his promise when I was sick.
Days and nights he watched over me.
He slept on the floor, wherever he could.
He talked to me twenty four hours a day.
He reassured me. He convinced me.
I would get better if only I would listen.
I finally listened. I feel better.
He is my healer. He is my husband.
I hope he keeps his promise forever.

Words

Our love is a serenade of words.
We share them with tranquility.
Their music is soft, entertaining.
How pleasurable it is to hear them.

A daily joy they bring to us.
Their sound is calm, intense.
An *everlasting* they convey. What a gift they are in our lives.

Words are for you and me, sanity.
They brighten the sky with their light.
Their music forms the past, the future.
When you and I are gone, our words will remain.

My Words

I know they are not perfect.
Sometimes they even disconnect.
For sure they are not always correct.
They often are unchecked.

He understands them right away.
He even plays with them every day.
He does not have to listen to them carefully.
Gently, he goes with the flow of my words.

It does not matter, their root.
There is always a path for their proof.
He jokes about them.
He cares for their stem.

For him my words mean something.
Usually their form is made of nothing.
He loves their French music.
I enjoy their fabric.

Comfy

Thank you for the blanket you placed over me yesterday.
I was not cold. I was not hot. I felt great.
It was an evening when everything was perfect.
The night was covering the sky on that end of Saturday.

I could have seen you approaching me slowly;
Placing this blanket on me delicately.
Being taken care of, I would have certainly
Wished to be next to you, but I was tired definitively.

Thank you for your thought of making me comfy.

When She Was Born, I Was Not Prepared

She was wanted and desired.
In my arms she cried.

I observed her.
I was not prepared.

I loved her right away.

I was scared.
I wanted to kiss her.

I touched her hands.
Her hands were small.

She was a doll but alive.
How would I take care of her?

I observed her.
I was not sure.

It was not the first baby I saw.
She was my first one.

She was life.
I now had responsibility for her.

Would I make it fine?

She grew up. I grew up.

I took care of her life.
I took care of my life.

Now I see her children grow up.

At The Lake

She gives me her hand.
I can feel it in mine.
She starts running.
I try to keep up with her.

"Grandma, Grandma, come!
I want to see the ducks.
Come, Grandma, come."
She runs faster and faster.

Suddenly, I put pressure
On her hand to let her know
That she must run slower.
We are at the lake now.

We sit next to each other.
We speak about the ducks.
She laughs, she screams,
She becomes agitated.

Innocently, she asks me,
"Can I go in the water?"
"No, my love, you cannot.
I am too old to rescue you."

We watch and feed the ducks.
At dusk, when tired,
I take her hand in mine.
We leave happy and hungry.

I Call Him my Son

I knew of the rich, the middleclass and the poor.
Bourgeois I was until that day I met him.
He was bright, thoughtful, well educated.
Art was his favorite subject.

Languages were his hobbies as well as travels.
It was interesting to have a conversation with him.
I discovered that he was different than I.
I was shocked at the beginning.
I just did not know what to think about him.

He showed me the world with his own eyes.
I loved it and I had to make a decision.
Was he good, bad or someone not to associate with?
Was he a person of concern for my children?
I had no idea what this young guy would teach us.

He invited me to his friend's houses.
They were alike. I loved them right away.
I was respected. I was neither confused nor scared.
My decision was made. We would be friends.

I have never regretted having him in my life.
He showed me his world. He transformed me.
One of my children could have been like him.
Would I then love my child less?

When you meet someone distinctive, you change.
He is not like the majority of people.
He is a son, a brother, a friend, a boyfriend.
And maybe he will get married soon.
People like him are seen as sinners.
Whom would I be to judge? I call him my son.

My Nephew

He was my Nephew
I knew him in my 50s,
though we never met in person.

He worked on a project in French.
My husband and I translated it into English.

Every day we spoke on the phone.
We were going to visit him.

One day he had an accident.
He fell with a box.
He was in a coma.

He left us.
We never met him.

My Writing Class is an Everyday Holiday

It is not a superficial knowledge.
I eat and drink from the words
I read and hear in class.

Comments are gratefully accepted.
Critique, goals, smiles, tears;
an exchange of universal thinking.

With my classmates, I grow.
My family, my husband,
and grandkids accept it.

I am becoming a woman.

Thank you to the class.
Happy Holidays!

The Creative English Writing Class

Here I was, lonely and lost in time.
I did not want to wake up.

My husband asked me to take the Creative English Writing
class.
I did not know what to expect.

I wrote my first piece with hesitation.
There was no inspiration within me.

I wrote about my life.
How would people react?

It was not something to tell to strangers.
I experienced the need to express myself more.

I could even read English in front of people.
I think I developed some new skills.

I socialized with a free mind. Our class was made of special
people.

We have all been through difficult times.
Our writing was shared with faith in others.

It started with us, our own experiences.
Most of us were shy at the beginning.

Today, it's easier to go on together.
We are the *Wednesday Group*.

We even do our weekly homework. I am well-awake and I
write.
It's a new day for me.

Our Wednesday Class

She cannot tell who she is.
Her emotions she has to keep.
We can all guess.
She has a vibrant nature.
Shyness is her virtue.
She needs to be strong.

Tears are often showing.
The mask disappears.
For a moment she forgets.

We listen to her carefully.
Our writing she critiques peacefully.
She is the living sea of our words.

We wait to see her weekly.
We are addicted to her.
She is our Wednesday class.
She is our English teacher.

Wondering

I am wondering
Why from a dream
It was great
To be like my friends

In that dream
I was laughing,
Talkative, ecstatic
It was in English

I was fluent-speaking
A woman like
The others known
In my Creative English Class

I was Anne Marie
The one I knew of
In France; jovial, open
Expressing ideas, feelings

So why cannot I be
Anne Marie the faithful
Speaking in English
When with people?

Or is my dream
The beginning
Of a new journey?

You Changed My Life

Yesterday, I was someone.
Today, I am different.

I wonder about you.
You are exquisite.

Selfishness is not you.
I love your creativity.

Your voice is unique.
You move like the wind.

People love you.
People listen to you.

You are their friend.
You are my friend.

Friendship

Friendship is about love.
We respect the one we speak to.
We don't want to know more.
We wait for the right moment.
We don't push the issue.
We listen to what is being said.
We don't judge.
We open our hearts.
We are not possessive.
We share consciously.
Friendship is being in a relationship.
We believe in each other.

Holidays

The miracle of life;
The written word
Becoming a story.

Testament:
Who we were,
Where we go,
Who we have become.

Creation:
A story told...
Emotions understood,
Feelings sensed.

Joy:
The delight of sharing
Each and every week
Our writing, on Thursdays.

Holidays:
The holidays are here.
We thank everyone Who helps us grow; shares our life.

Be

If I was knocking, would he open the door?
I need to wake up to his words.
There is one that strikes me:

Be

I am not yet.

I am she; *I am* her; *I am* you.
I have to figure out who the *I* in *I am* is.
Will I be able to do that soon?

Broken Heart

"You break my heart."
It's not uncommon to hear that.
Do we understand?
What a broken heart is?

Mine has been broken for years.
Not that I am the only one.
It could have, at any time
Stopped doing its work.

I grew up with songs of love.
My heart had the sound of love.
Then it became slower,
Because of the fears; the unexpected.

Today my heart still feels pain
When I try to open it with my friends.
I look for the Highest love of all, my faith.
To open it, feel it, build it again.

Today I am an apprentice.
I open my broken heart.
A man listened to me, married me.
With him I hear the songs of love again.

Chaos

Chaos: I have gone there, as numerous people have before me. Many more will surely follow. It can take years to get back into the driver's seat. It is good to understand where we come from and where we are going. I am gently moving toward that phase. My children are fine, my grandchildren are fine. My husband and I are going in the same direction. We want the best for each other. Peace moves closer and closer to surround us. I make beautiful friends. I love hugging people. It seems that they appreciate it. I am better understood here with my French education. It's a new me in America. My writing helps me to understand my former chaos and if I am not yet there to think for myself, I know I will be one day. I simply need to retrain my brain and continue to move forward for the best.

Our Home

The valley is below our home.
We can see it all around us.
It's a calm area where we live.
We would not have expected that.

When we were looking for a home, we visited this house last.
We knew it was for our family.
Sometimes you feel things.
You cannot explain why.

It's been years of hard work,
fun, education and growth.
Now that our kids have their own homes
our home is full of memories.

It's time for my husband and me
to think about ourselves.
We have achieved a lot in 20 years
And life should not end now.

Sunrise

I got up very early,
I could not see the sky.
The people were sleeping

Now it is the birth
of a new day and
the light is coming back.
The one that He
painted for us;
it's glory on earth.

Red, white, blue....
hills in the wilderness.
This is what I see at dawn.
It's magnificent.

Saint Valentine

The birds are singing.
Nature is flowering.
We contemplate the sky.

The streets are wild.
The cafés are full.
We dine together.

The teddy bears are white.
The hearts are red.
We kiss each other.

The movie theater is filled.
The cars are orderly.
We go home, delighted.

Long live Saint Valentine.

The Full Moon

It's very early in the morning.
The Santa Ana winds are blowing.
It must be cold outside.

It's there. It's full. It's luminous.
What I see is a circle in the sky.
I see nothing else above it.

The valley is sleeping.
It's time for me to go back to bed.
I look at the moon one more time.
I am wondering where the coyotes moved.

We have so many houses below ours.
It did not use to be that way.
Why did that happen?

It is still quiet. I should not complain.

The Pen, the Pain

The pen
The pain
I love your words
You world is tough
I love your sounds
Your silence is hard

The pen
The pain
I love your songs
Your bud is unkind
I love your music
Your hearing is harsh

The pen
The pain
I love your happiness
Your sorrow is hostile
I love your creativity
Your heart is cruel

The pen
The pain
It's Noel
Let the pain
Go away

The Waves

They face the south and the north.
They turn from the east to the west.

They encircle the world.
They initiate a dance.
All of it is a performance.

They have a pure desire to swirl.
Their behaviors are full of joy.
They are delicate.

They wrap and let go.
They are the stars on stage.

The Little Chapel

I am not a great cathedral
although I am very important.
I am not worried as in some big cities,
about the rain, the ice and the snow.

My life, I share
with splendid people
who are reliable and work
for my future.

I spend time with the carpenter, the painter and other great
men and women;
when the longest day
and the shorter come.

The volunteers are my self-esteem,
the visitors, my gladness.
When the people I love open, from time to time, my doors.

I am historical.

Paris in August

It was the full moon.
The stars embellished the sky.
The night was vibrant and full of life.
It was Paris on the Champs Elysees.

The terraces of the cafés,
the people walking hand in hand ...
the lights all around us,
It was Paris illuminated.

She is a dazzling city.
Her museums are full of history.
Her river, La Seine, is a beauty,
and her golden monuments, outstanding.

The boats in the river, her palaces of history,
bring me to my authentic history of France.
Her Cathedral Notre Dame de Paris
is marvelous.

Paris is my inheritance and universal beauty.
The kings and queens are part of her.
Her culture is formal and informal.
I want her to be that way for ever.

Made in the USA
Columbia, SC
16 November 2022

71366351R00080